Molly Oake

ALVIN **A**ILEY, JR.

ALVIN AILEY, JR.

A LIFE IN DANCE

JULINDA LEWIS-FERGUSON

Walker and Company
New York

First published in the United States of America in 1994
by Walker Publishing Company, Inc.

Published simultaneously in Canada by Thomas Allen & Son
Canada, Limited, Markham, Ontario

Library of Congress Cataloging-in-Publication Data
Lewis-Ferguson, Julinda.
Alvin Ailey, Jr.: a life in dance / Julinda Lewis-Ferguson.
p.   cm.
Includes bibliographical references (p.) and index.
ISBN 0-8027-8239-6. —ISBN 0-8027-8241-8 (library ed.)
1. Ailey, Alvin—Juvenile literature.   2. Dancers—United States—
Biography—Juvenile literature.   3. Choreographers—United States—
Biography—Juvenile literature.   I. Title.
GV1785.A38L48   1994
792.8'028'092-dc20
[B]   93-17906
CIP
AC

Book design by Claire Vaccaro

Printed in the United States of America
2   4   6   8   10   9   7   5   3   1

CONTENTS

ACKNOWLEDGMENTS

Many, many thanks to my editor, Henry Rasof; my husband, Ralph G. I. Ferguson; Alvin Ailey's mother, Mrs. Lula Elizabeth Cooper; A. Peter Bailey; Jack Vartoogian; Bill Hilton; Hakim Mutlaq; Michael Kaiser, Executive Director of the Alvin Ailey American Dance Center; Sylvia Waters, Director of the Ailey Repertory Ensemble; Barbara Strattnor and the staff of the New York Public Library at Lincoln Center; the staff of the Brooklyn Public Library Central Branch/Periodicals Room; Jennifer Dunning of *The New York Times* for her generous offer of research assistance; Ernestine Stodelle, who first encouraged me to write; Gary Parks, reviews editor at *Dance Magazine*; Dr. Robert LaPrince; my children, Jamila, Soleil Afafa, and Amandla; and to God who makes all things possible.

ALVIN AILEY, JR.

INTRODUCTION

Alvin Ailey, Jr., a choreographer, was an artist who created pictures in dance. Using movement, music, costumes, and lights, he created seventy-nine dances, the most famous of which, *Revelations*, is well known the world over. *Revelations* is a celebration of the African-American religious music of Ailey's rural Southern childhood. "Its roots are in American Negro culture, which is part of the whole country's heritage. But the dance speaks to everyone. . . . Otherwise it wouldn't work," Ailey said of his most popular work. Many young dancers, and dance lovers of all ages, came to know Ailey's work through *Revelations*.

Alvin Ailey never wanted to be labeled solely a "black artist," but he became one of the most widely known artists of his time to draw upon his African-American heritage for inspiration.

Donna Wood leads the company in the final section of *Revelations,* 1979 performance. (Photo by Jack Vartoogian)

Ailey's energetic and entertaining style of dancing introduced many African-Americans to modern dance. At the same time, it introduced other people to the art and culture of African-Americans. Ailey's powerful, exuberant movement routinely included unusual and exciting combinations of different styles of dancing, including ballet, modern dance, and jazz dancing.

Alvin Ailey formed his own dance company in 1958. Before that time, American modern dance was less popular than it came to be during the 1960s and 1970s. In its early days, modern dance was performed in small theaters and in concert halls. Sometimes it was presented in places that were not originally intended to be used for performances at all, such as the New York City YM–YWHA (the Young Men's and Young Women's Hebrew Association, the Jewish equivalent of the YMCA), where Ailey would present his first concert. Most early modern dance was performed for small audiences of faithful and devoted followers — often people who were dancers themselves.

Starting with an all-black company, and later working with an integrated group of black, white, and Asian dancers from the United States and around the world, Ailey made modern dance understandable. For this remarkable accomplishment, he was sometimes criticized for being too commercial, for turning high art (which only a few people could understand and like) into popular entertainment (which anyone could understand and like). "My dream was to provide a showcase for black material," Ailey recalled in a 1988 interview. He did that, and much more.

"THOSE BEAUTIFUL BLACK DANCERS"

On Saturday nights there was dancing at the Dew Drop Inn, the local hangout—perhaps the only hangout—for the black citizens of Rogers, Texas, a small town about fifty miles south of Waco. Besides dancing, it was a place for drinking Nehi soda pop and stronger beverages, and eating hot, sticky barbecue.

On Sunday morning, there were services at the True Vine Baptist Church, where young people attended Sunday school, worked with the Baptist Young People's Union, or went with their parents to meetings.

These were the chief activities, aside from attending school or going to work, for the black citizens of this typical small Texas town. And this was the life into which Alvin Ailey, Jr., was born to Alvin and Lula Elizabeth Ailey on January 5, 1931. Alvin was the fourteenth person in the household, which included his parents, his grandfather, an aunt and uncle, and eight cousins. When Alvin was about six months old, his father left the family, leaving Alvin and his mother, who was only seventeen, to make their own way in life. While growing up without a father in the home was not an ideal situation, it was not that unusual given the time and the place. America in the 1930s was in the depths of the Great Depression, a period of economic hardship that affected the whole country for the entire decade. Many black men, some of them fathers with families to take care of, were unable to find work and support their families. Some of these men left their homes to seek work. Some took odd jobs to survive. Some committed crimes and were sent to prison. Given the social climate and the economic hardships common to many black Americans at that time, it was not surprising that Alvin did not hear from his father for many years.

Alvin and his mother moved into their own small cabin on a large farm, and she supported them by washing and ironing white people's clothes. Mrs. Ailey grew vegetables for them in a small garden. They picked cotton in Wharton, Texas. And Mrs. Ailey worked as a live-in housekeeper for white families who could afford household help.

When Alvin was six years old, he and his mother moved to Navasota, Texas, where Mrs. Ailey was the first black woman to get a job in the local hospital.

Alvin made friends with a neighboring farmer and developed a fondness for animals. He had a pet dog and learned to ride a horse. By the time he was eight years old, he had developed an interest in drawing and often could be found sketching insects and writing in a notebook that he carried everywhere. When Alvin demonstrated a gift for music, he was able to take music lessons at school and learned to play the tuba.

In many small towns or rural communities in the South (but in some other parts of the United States as well), segregation was the rule and often the law. Segregation meant that people of different colors had to be kept separate. Whites and blacks lived in separate neighborhoods and attended different schools. Movie theaters, department stores, parks, playgrounds, and restaurants were segregated, too. There were separate entrances for whites and blacks, separate water fountains, separate rest rooms. In movie theaters, blacks usually sat in the balcony.

"There was the white school up on the hill, and the black Baptist church and the segregated theaters and neighborhoods. Like most of my generation, I grew up feeling like an outsider, like someone who didn't matter," Ailey remembered in a December 1988 interview for the *New York Daily News Magazine*. But this was not the life Mrs. Ailey wanted for her son.

In 1942, after finishing the school year in Texas, where he stayed with friends of the family, Alvin joined his mother in Los Angeles. She had gotten a

Alvin Ailey, about age fourteen, shortly after moving to California. Shown here with his stepfather, Mr. Fred W. Cooper, about 1945–46.

(Courtesy of Mrs. Lula Elizabeth Cooper)

well-paying job in an aircraft factory there. Alvin was twelve years old.

It was about this time that he was first exposed to concert dance—dance meant to be performed before an audience. He went on a trip with his Valencia Junior High class to see a performance of a famous dance company from Europe, the Ballet Russe de Monte Carlo. The company, performing at the Los Angeles Philharmonic Hall, danced two well-known and popular ballets, *L'Après-midi d'un faune* (*The Afternoon of a Faun*) and *Schéhérazade*. The first was a daringly different fairy-tale ballet by the great Russian dancer and choreographer Vaslav Nijinsky; the other was a colorful spectacle by choreographer Mikhail Fokine, also Russian.

Soon after, in 1945, Ailey saw the Katherine Dunham Dance Company perform at Los Angeles's Biltmore Theater. This was a troupe of black dancers under the direction of Katherine Dunham, a remarkable woman who was not only a dancer but also a choreographer, actress, writer, producer, composer, educator, and anthropologist.

Dunham's dances, choreographed largely between 1938 and 1950, were performed on Broadway stages and in Hollywood productions as well as on the concert stage. Dunham herself was such a great beauty and gifted dancer that her legs were rumored to be insured for a million dollars by Lloyd's of London, the international insurance market famous for its exotic policies.

Dunham also developed a unique technique—a dance technique is a specific way of training dancers; it usually consists of a series of exercises and short movements whose execution creates a specific style and flavor. Dunham's technique was based on isolation—that is, on moving specific body parts, such as the head or shoulder, alone. The dancer then progresses to performing different rhythms or movements with different body parts at the same time. This is a different method of movement than traditional ballet, in which the dancing body aims to create simple lines and an airy, elevated look. The Dunham technique used parallel feet, rather than the turned-out positions of ballet, and featured body rolls, which start from the base of the spine and with the back parallel to the floor, rather than erect. Dunham dancers danced on flat feet, instead of on their toes, again quite unlike ballet dancers. They would move across the floor with slightly bent knees, their shoulders moving up and down, front and back, and then in complete circles.

Isolation came from what Dunham called "primitive movements"—the movements of Caribbean fieldwork dances, of African ritual dances, of fighting dances. Watching the Dunham company in performance made a deep and lasting impression on Ailey. Together with his childhood memories of Sunday school and church services, and the music of both the church and the off-limits dance hall, the influence of Katherine Dunham would emerge in many of the works Ailey would later create. In fact, one of Ailey's greatest projects before his death was a full-evening length program in tribute to this great figure in American dance.

But Dunham and her exciting choreography were not the greatest influence on Ailey's art. He later recalled, "I was completely hooked from the moment I saw those beautiful black dancers doing dances taken from all over the world."

Alvin had been intrigued, stimulated, and entertained by the performances he had seen, and he was very athletic, but he had still not been moved to actually dance.

''ALL THOSE THINGS WE SAW AT THE CLUB ALABAMA''

A lvin Ailey's career as a dancer began in Los Angeles, with Lester Horton, one of the pioneers of American modern dance. Ted Crumb, a high school friend, took Ailey to the Horton school. Ailey decided to enroll in the school, where he would learn one of the major modern-dance techniques. But what, exactly, is modern dance, and what makes it an important American art form? To understand this, we must first look briefly at ballet.

Ballet, one of the theater arts, is a style of dancing developed for performance, rather than for recreation. Originally, ballet was pretty much a social form of dance, just as the Charleston was in America in the 1920s, or the jitterbug or lindy hop was in the 1950s, or the electric slide is today.

But ballet dancing has specific movements and positions—a "vocabulary of movements"—that have been modified and perfected over hundreds of years. Traditional ballet movements are always based on five positions. As these movements and positions became more and more specific, requiring ever greater skill of the performer, ballet became very specialized. Eventually it became something only a few people performed, while others watched.

Modern dance, on the other hand, grew not from social dancing but from the desire of individuals who were already dancers and creative artists to more freely express themselves. These dancers felt that the specialized movements of ballet dancing did not meet their creative needs. Modern dancers wanted the freedom to *choose* their movements and poses. In recent times, modern dancers have experimented with simple, everyday movements, such as standing and staring at the audience, or even not moving at all!

Modern dance has always represented something new, different, even rebellious. It developed largely in the United States, beginning in the early 1900s. The first major modern dance company in America, that of Ruth St. Denis and Ted Shawn, began in 1915—at least fifteen years before the first American ballet companies were formed in the 1930s.

Lester Horton formed his dance company in 1932. He opened his own dance school and theater, the Lester Horton Dance Theater, in Hollywood, in 1946.

This theater is believed to have been the first in the United States to be devoted exclusively to dance. Horton's company performed there year round, on weekends. Most significantly for Alvin Ailey, Lester Horton's dance company was the first in the United States to be racially integrated. African-American, Mexican-American, and Japanese-American dancers, among others, were accepted as equals.

Horton demanded a lot from his dancers. Although he found ballet an unsatisfactory medium through which to express his ideas, he encouraged his dancers to study ballet as well as modern dance in order to have a wide range of movements in their dance vocabulary. Horton dancers also studied drama, painting, and sculpture. They learned how to read music, to operate the sound system and the lights in the theater, to sew costumes, to build scenery, and to construct props.

Ailey studied the full Horton curriculum, but he also pursued a college education. While a scholarship student at the Lester Horton Dance Theater, he attended the University of California at Los Angeles; in 1949 he transferred to San Francisco State College. During this period, he met and was influenced by the life and work of Maya Angelou, an African-American woman writer. He also performed for a while with a touring nightclub act under the direction of Lou Fonteyne. He then returned to the Horton school to complete his rigorous training and apprenticeship. Ailey made rapid progress with Horton but was too shy to come onstage for what was to have been his first performance. He eventually overcame his stage fright and grew into an excellent dancer with a commanding presence.

Horton required that his dancers communicate well through movement, that they have strength and endurance, and that they use the full range of space, tempo, rhythm, and emotions available to them. All of these elements would later become important in Alvin Ailey's work as well. Many years later Ailey would recall this time of learning with Horton and say, "It gave me a great sense of self-esteem to see that Lester thought the Lindy, the Shake dances . . . all those things we saw at the Club Alabama—were worthwhile."

Horton brought his company east in 1953 for their first and only performance in New York, just a few months before he died suddenly of a heart attack. The company had been engaged to perform through 1954. Upon Horton's death, the company was left without a director or choreographer and faced the prospect of disbanding. Out of respect for Horton, Ailey, a young man in his early twenties with a love of dancing and a growing interest in choreography, took over as artistic director of the company.

Faced with the leadership of a dance company, Ailey began to choreograph his own works. In 1953 he choreographed *According to Saint Francis* for the Lester

Horton Dancers, in tribute to Horton. The dance, Ailey's first work, was thirty-seven minutes long. It was so demanding that the soloist, James Truitte, lost more than ten pounds during the rehearsals and performances. In 1954, Ailey followed his first attempt with *Mourning, Morning*, based on themes from plays by Tennessee Williams, and *Creation of the World*, which depicted what some would call a primitive version of the Adam and Eve creation story. The works did not receive good reviews, but the company needed new dances, and Ailey was eager to try.

The Horton company returned to the Jacob's Pillow Dance Festival in western Massachusetts during the summer of 1954, under the direction of the still-inexperienced Alvin Ailey. Ted Shawn, the festival's director, was not impressed with Alvin Ailey's work. Later that same year, Ailey and another Lester Horton dancer, his friend Carmen de Lavallade, were invited to New York to dance in the Broadway show *House of Flowers*. This was an important turning point in Alvin Ailey's career.

CHAPTER THREE

BIRTH OF A DANCE COMPANY

When Alvin Ailey came to the Broadway stage he found the perfect combination of people and opportunity to help realize his dreams. The Hollywood choreographer Herbert Ross had been given the job of choreographing the Broadway play *House of Flowers*, written by the well-known American writer Truman Capote. Ross had used Alvin Ailey and Carmen de Lavallade in the RKO film *Carmen Jones*, an adaptation of the opera *Carmen*. *Carmen Jones*, adapted by Oscar Hammerstein II and set to music by Bizet, was a musical with an all-black cast. Adaptations of plays that were not originally written for black characters were common, and provided work for African-American actors, singers, and dancers. The theater and film industries were largely segregated in the 1950s, and interracial casts were rare and often controversial.

Ross remembered how well Ailey and de Lavallade had danced together in Hollywood and offered them featured parts in the play. The two dancers arrived in Philadelphia in December 1954 to prepare for out-of-town performances. Traditionally, Broadway plays are first presented out of town in preparation for the formal Broadway opening.

Some of the best black dancers in America were involved in this production, including Louis Johnson, the first black dancer to perform with the New York City Ballet, and Arthur Mitchell, the first black male ballet star in the New York City Ballet. Curiously, Mitchell, who at that time had much more dance experience than Ailey, was Ailey's understudy.

House of Flowers drew a lot of attention for the performers. The stage—decorated with sunflower vines, a gramophone shaped like a morning glory, and a red-fringed hammock—made quite an impression. In writing about black American performers, reviewers commonly described them as "wild," "grotesque," "animalistic," "novel," "primitive," or "pagan." The men were often described by stereotyped images of savages, lazy do-nothings, or sexually promiscuous ne'er-do-wells. The women were either overweight mother figures or seductresses. These attitudes prolonged segregation in the theater arts and prevented the work of black Americans from being taken seriously. Some of the favorable reviews reflected such sentiments and would now be considered prejudiced.

Critic Brooks Atkinson of *The New York Times* wrote, "Every Negro show includes wonderful dancing. *House of Flowers* is no exception. Tall and short Negroes, adults and youngsters, torrid maidens in flashy costumes and bare-chested bucks break out into a number of wild, grotesque, animalistic dances."

John Chapman of the *New York Daily News* wrote, "There is a dance devised and performed by Geoffrey Holder which is a weird and fascinating novelty."

Carmen de Lavallade was singled out by *New York Journal-American* writer George Jean Nathan as follows:

> *The dances have also been criticized as deficient in novel patterns. I say spinach and the hell with it. True enough, they are the wild, disordered brand but thus exactly serve the nature and mood of the show. . . . The dances in their pagan fury are what the show calls for, and they are sensuously thrilling, as in the Mardi Gras number which includes a delightful new dancing girl, Carmen de Lavallade, and, in the way of humor, the exhausted morning-after number danced by the "students."*

After performing in the successful run of *House of Flowers*, Ailey remained in New York City. It was 1955, and then as now, New York City was the dance center of the United States, if not the world. Ailey was a tall, handsome young man of twenty-four. Stocky and muscular, he sometimes thought he was too big to be a dancer, but he studied and participated in workshops at the New Dance Group, an exciting creative center for modern dance. There, he worked with leading choreographer Anna Sokolow and performed in her well-known dramatic dance *Rooms*, a piece about isolation, performed to jazz-band music. He danced in Donald McKayle's *Games*, a dance that expresses the underlying feelings of fear in the street games of urban children. He studied dance at the Martha Graham school with Doris Humphrey, and with Hanya Holm and Charles Weidman. He also took classes with the famous acting teacher Stella Adler and studied at the Karel Shook Dance School. (Karel Shook was the ballet master who, with Arthur Mitchell, founded the Dance Theatre of Harlem.) And after class, alone at home, Ailey practiced the steps he had learned.

Alvin Ailey, in costume for an acting role, probably that of the Chinese Bandit in *The Carefree Tree*, about 1955. (Courtesy of Mrs. Lula Elizabeth Cooper)

While studying dance and theater in New York, Ailey won a number of acting roles and directing assignments. He performed in several Broadway and off-Broadway theatrical productions. In 1955, he played the role of a Chinese bandit in *The Carefree Tree*, a play about a young Chinese soldier married to a beautiful princess; they prevent a war and triumph over seemingly insurmountable obstacles to live happily ever after.

In 1956 Ailey appeared in the musical production *Sing, Man, Sing*, with the well-known singer Harry Belafonte. Mary Hinkson, a prominent black female dancer who performed with Martha Graham's company during this period, was a featured dancer in *Sing, Man, Sing*. Walter Nicks, who had danced in *House of Flowers* with Ailey, was the choreographer.

In New York Ailey continued his friendship with Carmen de Lavallade, but their partnership ended in 1956 following her marriage to Geoffrey Holder. Ailey's new partner was dancer Christyne Lawson.

While performing with the Horton company in California, Ailey had caught the attention of the choreographer Jack Cole. Cole had been impressed enough to choreograph parts for Ailey, Carmen de Lavallade, and Claude Thompson in a film called *Lydia Bailey*. (However, Ailey never actually appeared in the completed film.) In 1957, Ailey and Christyne Lawson auditioned before Cole for roles in the musical *Jamaica*, of which Cole was the choreographer.

Written by the team of E. Y. Harburg and Fred Saidy, the musical depicted the fictitious Pigeon Island, off the coast of Jamaica. Lena Horne, the leading African-American singer and actress of that time, starred as Savannah, who wanted more than anything to go to New York. Ricardo Montalban, best known later for his popular television role on "Fantasy Island," played Savannah's fisherman boyfriend, Koli, who wanted to stay right where he was. The show received mixed reviews—apparently the story line was not as good as some might have liked—but most critics agreed that Horne was a true star and that Cole's choreography was superb. On another note, a feature story about *Jamaica* in *Variety*, a major show-business publication, focused on the ever-present issue of racism. A staff writer named Hobe wrote:

> *There may be various reactions to the racial aspect of the show. Although most northern urbanites aren't likely to be concerned (most New Yorkers probably couldn't care less), there may be raised eyebrows and perhaps increased blood pressure among Dixiecrats because of the love scenes between Miss Horne [who is black] and Montalban [who is Mexican], even though the latter appears to have been sun-lamped considerably. . . . The dialog and lyrics are utterly noncommittal on the race and color of the hero.*

On the social front, *Jamaica* may have been ahead of its time. It opened in New York in October 1957, and in spite of the mixed reaction of the professional critics, the show was a success and enjoyed a long run.

In 1960, Alvin Ailey choreographed a production of *Dark of the Moon*, a play by Howard Richardson and William Claibourne Berney. The play was produced by Vinette Carroll, a leading name in black theater, and the cast was packed with the best black performers available.

The next year, Ailey performed his first dramatic role, in Michael Shurtleff's play *Call Me By My Rightful Name*. The stars of the play were well-known actors Robert Duvall and Joan Hackett. Ailey played the role of a young black man named Paul who was involved in a confrontation with his white college roommate concerning a white girl both had befriended. Richard Watts, Jr., writing in the *New York Post*, considered the play "an honest, thoughtful and probing study of the racial tensions potentially present even among men of good will."

In that same year, Ailey played a boxer in *Two By Saroyan* and had a major dramatic role in the play *Tiger, Tiger, Burning Bright*, with actresses Claudia McNeill and Diana Sands. Ailey played Clarence, the son who quit his job with the telegraph company to make his living as a thief and live off wealthy white women.

Ailey received considerable acclaim for his work. The *New York Times* writer Howard Taubman praised the "effective performances by Alvin Ailey as the tigerish son whose ways are furtive." Thomas R. Dash in *Women's Wear Daily* wrote: "Alvin Ailey catches the ferocity of the surly, perverted, and tigerish Clarence." But not all the reviews were kind to Ailey. In *The Village Voice*, Michael Smith wrote that "leading man [Alvin Ailey] gives [Diana Sands] nothing to play against."

Ailey continued to work in theater even after his own company was well established. In 1964 he codirected *Jericho–Jim Crow*, a play by the famous poet and writer Langston Hughes. The play used songs, including spirituals, to trace the history of blacks in the United States, from Africa to slavery to the 1963 march on Washington. *New York Morning Telegraph* critic Whitney Bolton wrote that "Alvin Ailey and [codirector] William Hairston have directed with spirit; the production is, as it should have been, kept simple."

But all of this theater work was beside Ailey's main goal. Throughout this period, he continued to study dance, to choreograph, and occasionally to perform as a dancer. It was the 1957 production of *Jamaica* that, indirectly, presented Ailey with a big opportunity. He took advantage of it.

Jamaica provided Ailey and the other dancers with more than just a steady job and a regular income, although these things were certainly important to them. It also gave them the economic security they needed to pursue their own interests. During their time off, and when the theater was not in use, those dancers who had an interest in choreography were able to work on their own ideas. Those dancers who wanted more opportunities to dance offered their talent, their skills, and their bodies to those who wanted to create.

Ailey and Ernest Parham, another dancer who also had an interest in choreography, began working with just such a group of dancers. The dancers came from the chorus of *Jamaica*; from *Bells Are Ringing*, a musical starring Judy Holliday, in which Ernest Parham was appearing; from the former cast of *House of Flowers*; and from other musicals. There were about thirty-five dancers involved. They all worked together to prepare for an upcoming concert at the 92nd Street Y.

The YM–YWHA, located at Ninety-second Street on New York City's East Side, had become a well-known showcase for modern dance and the works of new choreographers. Dancers, choreographers, and dance critics all regularly attended the many performances at the 92nd Street Y's Kaufmann Auditorium, to see what was new, to get new ideas for movement, and to enjoy the wide variety of dance performed there.

In preparation for their performance, the dancers rehearsed at a place called Michael's Studio, which was convenient to the various Broadway theaters in which they were performing. The dancers would rehearse for several hours during the day and then later that same night go to the nearby theaters where they worked and dance some more.

Ailey prepared a long solo for himself, *Ode and*

Homage, dedicated to the memory of Lester Horton. A writer for *Dance Magazine* thought *Ode and Homage* "revealed a lack of experience" but also "had an inherent nobility." The dancers also performed *Redonda (Five Dances on Latin Themes)*. The program closed with *Blues Suite*, the first of many Ailey dances that would present various aspects of African-American culture to a general audience in a positive, artistic manner. In a note from the original program, Ailey summarized the many forces that inspired *Blues Suite*:

> *The musical heritage of the southern Negro remains a profound influence on the music of the world. . . . During the dark days the blues sprang full-born from the docks and the fields, saloons and bawdy houses . . . indeed from the very souls of their creators.*

Simply put, *Blues Suite* is a dance about the sounds and the feelings of the blues. In developing this dance, Ailey presented a portrait of American black culture, drawing on his own roots in Texas and on his memories of growing up and overcoming hard times. He also demonstrated how black people had been able to take something bad—poverty, depression, and hard times—and create from the experience something beautiful: an original style of music, the blues, that became a part of popular American culture enjoyed by all.

The performance was considered a success and was

well received by the audience. It brought offers for future performances. But little is known of what became of Ailey's partner, Ernest Parham. He presented two works on this program, *Trajectories* and *Icarus*. Yet although Parham shared in the positive reviews, all the attention was focused on Alvin Ailey. And there the attention would remain for quite some time.

PRESENTING THE ALVIN AILEY AMERICAN DANCE THEATER, ''IN WHICH MEN ARE MEN AND THE WOMEN ARE FRANKLY DELIGHTED ABOUT IT''

L ittle did Ailey suspect that that first performance at the 92nd Street Y would be the start of a thirty-year career. It is unlikely that Ailey had any intention of establishing a permanent company at this early date. Directing a company, as he well knew from his apprenticeship with and subsequent leadership of the Lester Horton dancers, was a difficult job. It was like being the father of a large family that required a home and emotional and financial support.

Rehearsal space—somewhere for the choreographers and dancers to prepare their work—had to be found. Dancers often were not paid for rehearsal time, but the musicians who worked with them had to be, as did landlords. Materials for costumes, props, and scenery had to be bought, costumes had to be sewn and stage sets built. Running a dance company requires an enormous amount of behind-the-scenes preparation and planning that is invisible to the audience.

It is not unusual for dancers to practice for months for the opportunity to perform in one of the many short-lived weekend programs, such as those produced at the 92nd Street Y. Many dancers hold other jobs, working for other choreographers, doing office work, or working in restaurants. Some are writers or teachers. Some attend school.

Some of Ailey's dancers were employed in Broadway shows. They would rehearse with Ailey for up to three hours a day, then race to their other jobs. The group would disband after completing a performance or series of performances, and the dancers would start the whole hectic routine all over again when a new program was being developed.

In 1958, money was not readily available to support the arts. (As dance became more popular in the 1960s and 1970s, government and private grants became more widely available to choreographers and dance companies.) But given the economic conditions of the time, many dancers performed on bare stages, with little or no scenery, and often wore simple black leotards or other nondescript clothing. Ailey had been influenced by the total theatrical experience of Lester Horton and by the colorful costumes and spectacular staging of Katherine Dunham's dancers. So Ailey and Geoffrey Holder constructed costumes from old curtains and from items found in used-clothing stores. They made stage decor and props from other found materials, things for which other people had little use anymore. Friends, rather than professional designers, helped with the sewing.

Yet none of these difficulties kept Ailey from soon preparing for a second concert, also at the 92nd Street Y. This, the first to feature a full evening of Ailey's own works, took place on December 21, 1958. The successful *Blues Suite* was on the program once again, along with *Cinco Latinos*, which was a suite of Latin dances. There was also a new work for featured guest artist Carmen de Lavallade called *Ariette Oubliée*. Critic P. W. Manchester wrote about this second performance in the February 1959 issue of *Dance News*.

> *After so many modern dance performances in which dancers drift about with blank faces and a general neutralization that denies the existence of sex even in the midst of the most complex entwinings, how refreshing to enter the stage world created by Alvin Ailey, in which the men are men and the women are frankly delighted about it.*

As a result of these two successes, Ailey's group was invited to perform at the Jacob's Pillow Dance Festival during the summer of 1959. Just five years before, an inexperienced Ailey had failed to impress the festival's director after taking over the direction of the Horton company. This time, with more experience and several good reviews to his credit, he met with more success. With things going so well, a third concert at the 92nd Street Y was planned for January 31, 1960.

The dancers were still not a formal company; many performers came and went as their work schedules allowed. Dancers would carry costumes and props about with them as they moved from one temporary rehearsal space to another. When the group began a tour of the eastern United States, bringing Ailey's dances to new audiences, friends loaded their cars with dancers, costumes, props, lights, and whatever else was needed to set up a performance. The idea of a permanent company, a showcase primarily for the works of black choreographers, was beginning to take shape.

For the January 1960 performance at the 92nd Street Y, the Ailey dancers continued the Latin theme of *Redondo* and *Cinco Latinos* with a Latin American suite called *Sonera*. *Sonera* consisted of three dances that attempted to combine ballet and ethnic dance forms. The group also performed *La Création du monde* ("The Creation of the World"), which Ailey had originally choreographed in 1954 for the Lester Horton dancers. But the most talked-about work on the program was the new *Revelations*.

Ailey used images from both personal experience

and the book of Revelations in the Bible. These are most apparent in the baptism scene and in the final section, when the church ladies, in their wide-brimmed hats, use their fans to communicate and to flirt as well as to gain relief from the oppressive Southern heat. The skills Ailey had learned under the tutelage of Lester Horton, the inspiration he had received from watching the works of Katherine Dunham, and the traditional music he had grown up hearing in the black church all helped Ailey present a story from the African-American cultural experience. He stunned and delighted his audience.

Originally performed in three parts, the dance opened with "Pilgrim of Sorrow," which featured a wedge-shaped formation of dancers, hands outstretched in a way that symbolizes both humble prayer and hope. Two long strips of fabric were unfurled across the stage to represent the water in a riverside baptism scene, "Take Me to the Water." The dancers' fluid movements made them appear to be floating. Simply adorned white umbrellas and long, slender poles or reeds with scraps of fabric rippling in the breeze made by the flitting dancers provide an elegant, festive atmosphere while not requiring elaborate sets and expensive materials. These tricks of the trade were influenced by Horton and necessity. The final scene, "Move, Members, Move," had ladies in Sunday hats vigorously fanning themselves in a fond parody of the black Southern Baptist church.

Opening scene from *Revelations,* 1979 performance. (Photo by Jack Vartoogian)

By most accounts, even at this first performance of *Revelations* the audience began to clap along with the music. At the end they stood up and cheered and demanded more. This type of enthusiastic audience reaction apparently was rather unusual at the 92nd Street Y. Ailey's dancers were scheduled for a return engagement—something that was unheard-of at the time—the very next month. Reviews and word of mouth spread the news of this exciting work. Alvin Ailey was no longer an unknown new choreographer. But his fledgling company—the Alvin Ailey American Dance Theater—still had no place to call home.

In 1960, the YWCA on Fifty-first Street and Eighth Avenue opened the Clark Center for the Performing Arts in the former Capitol Hotel. Charles Blackwell, a friend of Ailey's who was then the stage manager for *Jamaica*, had seen Ailey's rehearsals and was impressed. He approached Adele Holtz, the director of the Clark Center, and told her about Ailey's work. By October of that year, Holtz had been persuaded of the company's potential. Ailey's group became the Clark Center's resident dance company.

The company now had a home, a place to study and rehearse, a place to meet and plan, a place to store its costumes and props, and a place to grow. In exchange for their space, Ailey and his company members taught dance classes to children and adults and held seminars at which interested people could learn more about dance and choreography. And the center included a little theater where Ailey and other choreographers presented their work. Now people could really begin to take notice.

In 1962, the Alvin Ailey American Dance Theater was selected to be a part of the President's Special International Program for Cultural Presentations. Established by President Kennedy, this program was somewhat like the Peace Corps, which Kennedy had established in 1961 to promote world peace and friendship. While the Peace Corps brought education and skills to underdeveloped countries, the cultural program aimed to encourage understanding of other people's cultures, with the goal of working toward world peace.

For their first tour, the company was sent to perform in Southeast Asia and Australia for about thirteen weeks. The dancers were constantly on the move and had very little time to see much of the places they visited. But the audiences, even those who spoke different languages and those who had never before seen black Americans performing on the concert dance stage, were full of praise for the dancers and for Ailey's choreography.

It was not unusual for black American artists to receive greater acclaim in foreign countries than they did in the United States. Other African-American dancers, musicians, writers, and visual artists had moved to Europe in order to achieve recognition for their work and escape the racism they faced in their own country.

During the 1962–63 performing season, Ailey's company went to Brazil. In 1964, the company toured various colleges around the United States, visited Paris and London in their first tour of Europe, and then returned to Australia, representing the U.S. Department of State. Word of the group's success in Europe and Australia reached home and increased the company's popularity. In 1965 they went back to Europe; then again in 1966, only to get stranded in Italy when some performances were canceled and the group ran out of money. Through some hastily made arrangements, they were able to leave Italy and go to Senegal, in West Africa, where they represented the United

THE ALVIN AILEY AMERICAN DANCE THEATRE

Members of the Alvin Ailey American Dance Theater posing in costume for *Blues Suite*, Paris, 1964, include Alvin Ailey, reclining. (Uncredited press photo)

States in the First World Festival of Negro Arts in Dakar. The group toured West Africa the following year.

All this touring meant the dancers had more work, and the company became more permanent. Dancers no longer left after each performance or series of performances to return to full-time jobs. Dancing became their full-time job, with shorter and shorter periods of unemployment between the performances and touring engagements. When the company was at home, many of the troupe's members taught dance classes at Clark Center or at other dance schools.

Ailey was now being hired or commissioned to choreograph dances for other companies. In 1962 he created *Feast of Ashes* for the Joffrey Ballet. Four years later he created three works for the Harkness ballet, *Ariadne*, *Macumba*, and *El Amor brujo*. In 1966 he also choreographed *Anthony and Cleopatra* for the reopening of the Metropolitan Opera House at Lincoln Center in New York City.

As Ailey grew in stature as an artist, he was able to collaborate on projects with other artists whose works he admired or had been inspired by. In 1963 he began collaborating with the great jazz composer Duke Ellington on *The River*, a work commissioned by American Ballet Theater. He also worked with Ellington on the dance *Reflections in D*.

In the midst of all this creativity and traveling, Ailey remained aware of what was happening in the world around him. One of the plays in which he performed in 1961, *Call Me By My Rightful Name*, dealt with the issue of racism.

In June 1963 the Ailey company performed a benefit concert for the Southern Christian Leadership Conference, which worked for civil rights in the South. In 1964, while touring the southern United States, Ailey's company had to be careful to avoid the Ku Klux Klan, an organization that, among other activities, was working to prevent black Americans from registering to vote. "All my work, to some extent or other, is a cry against racism, against the injustice of that period," Ailey said in a December 1988 interview for the *New York Daily News Magazine*.

By the mid-1960s, Alvin Ailey was in his thirties and had become a well-respected choreographer whose responsibilities as the director of a popular dance company left him with little time to dance himself. In addition, he was a cultural ambassador, bringing American art to America's foreign friends. He had amassed a number of impressive credits both on Broadway and off, and he created works for other companies. Now, he began to focus more of his time and attention on choreography and on the administrative details of his growing organization.

''DANCE RIOT IN BROOKLYN''

Having a dance company. That is the great struggle, that has been the challenge of 30 years. Keeping it all together is still the problem, the constant battle to afford the engagements, the designers, the choreographers, to pay the dancers a decent wage. You have to keep proving that you have a right to exist. Even after all this time, I still have the feeling that it's not permanent, that at any moment something might happen.
— Alvin Ailey, 1988

I n 1967, Ailey's business manager, Ivy Clarke, helped create the Dance Theater Foundation, a nonprofit organization whose purpose was to help the company secure public and private funding. By 1968, the Alvin Ailey American Dance Theater had received grants from the privately endowed Rockefeller

Alvin Ailey, 1986. (Photo by
Jack Vartoogian)

Foundation and from the publicly funded National
Endowment for the Arts.

In 1969, the company moved across the river from
Manhattan to Brooklyn and became the resident dance
company of the Brooklyn Academy of Music, an established arts center that boasted three theaters plus
plenty of rehearsal space and office space. Stability was
once again a possibility, and the move enabled the formation of the Ailey company school.

A June 18, 1969, press release titled "Dance Riot in
Brooklyn" describes the beginnings of Ailey's school,
the American Dance Center: "Alvin Ailey, in association with the Brooklyn Academy of Music and with
the cooperation of the Hanson Place Central Methodist

Church has been conducting, since the first of May, free dance instruction for children and young adults of the local Brooklyn area."

One hundred twenty-five students registered for classes the first week. One instructor was assigned to teach three classes per week, but by the sixth week there were 400 students, and two more instructors had to be added. The Hanson Place Central Methodist Church, located near the Brooklyn Academy of Music, donated space for the classes. Capezio, a ballet-shoe maker and manufacturer of clothing for dance, donated tights and leotards for the students. The program was publicized as "a means of relating dance and its disciplines and the joy of movement to the lives of . . . young people."

The founding of a dance school established Ailey even more firmly as a major force in modern dance. Like Ruth St. Denis, Ted Shawn, Martha Graham, Katherine Dunham, and his mentor, Lester Horton, before him, Ailey was able to use his school not only as a source of dancers for his own company, but also as a center for arts education that would reach far beyond the boundaries of his own work.

In 1970 the Alvin Ailey American Dance Theater performed in Russia (which was then part of the Soviet Union). At the time, relations between the United States and the Soviet Union were not good. The Soviet Union had a long history of classical ballet, and the last dance company to visit that country had been a ballet company. But no modern dancer had performed there since Isadora Duncan, more than forty years earlier. More than ever, the Ailey dancers were cultural ambassadors when they toured the Soviet Union: They represented the best the American people had to offer. Soviet society was very closed at that time. Soviet citizens were rarely allowed to leave their country, and Westerners were not allowed to travel freely. Although there was a language barrier, Ailey's group was met with filled auditoriums and cheers that could be understood in any language. After one performance in Leningrad (St. Petersburg), the company received a standing ovation that lasted more than twenty minutes.

In January 1971 the Ailey company performed at the City Center Theater in New York City, and was such a hit that it was asked to return in three months. The highlight of the January performances was a fifteen-minute solo called *Cry*.

Ailey choreographed *Cry* for Judith Jamison's particular physique, style, and abilities. A tall, striking woman with graceful arms and long legs, Jamison was the best known of all the Ailey dancers. *Cry* was a tribute to Ailey's mother, whose birthday came during the performing season, and whom Ailey wanted to honor. He dedicated the dance to "all black women everywhere—especially our mothers." The dance accentuated Jamison's long arms and legs as they whipped the air with wild, exuberant energy. Dressed in a long white skirt and a scarf that could be put to many uses

Judith Jamison in Alvin Ailey's *Cry*, a dance created for her, in honor of his mother, Mrs. Lula Elizabeth Cooper, 1978 performance. (Photo by Linda Vartoogian)

as the dance developed, Jamison brought Ailey's ideas to life. She made *Cry* one of the most popular dances in the company's repertoire, and at the same time propelled herself into the spotlight of stardom.

Cry was one of the most difficult works Jamison ever had to perform. "I didn't know how difficult the dance was until opening night," she later recalled, "because we never got a chance to run it from beginning to end until the curtain went up." By popular demand, she performed *Cry* in twenty-six consecutive performances that year.

In May 1971, the company moved into the Fifty-

ninth Street studios, which choreographer Pearl Lang
had offered to share. This space, on Fifty-ninth Street
in Manhattan, was much closer to the heart of the
dance world and the major theaters than the Brooklyn
Academy of Music. Ailey's school, which had attracted
many students in Brooklyn, continued to grow in its
new location. The staff was increased, with some of the
best teachers available in classical ballet, Horton, Dunham, and Graham techniques. Pearl Lang, while still
leading her own dance company, became the artistic
director of the Alvin Ailey American Dance Center,
the company's official school.

During these hectic years of popularity, Ailey
earned several prestigious awards for his choreography.
Among them were the Gold Star for Best Modern
Dance Company (1970), the Dance Magazine Award
(1975), the Springarn Medal, awarded by the NAACP
(1979), and the Capezio Award (1979).

Alvin Ailey and friend and
former partner, Carmen
de Lavallade, share a slice
of anniversary cake at the
gala celebrating the
company's twentieth
anniversary, 1978. (Photo by
Jack Vartoogian)

In 1974 Ailey created a second company, the Alvin Ailey Repertory Ensemble. By its twentieth anniversary in 1978, the Alvin Ailey American Dance Theater was one of the most popular dance companies in America. Many former dancers and old friends returned to celebrate Ailey's success because, as hard as he worked, he had never done so solely for his own benefit.

LOOKING TO THE FUTURE

Even in the early days of the company, Ailey was committed to two important missions: preserving important dances of the past, and encouraging and supporting the development of young and emerging talent. At the same time, he continued to follow his own creative vision, making dances and directing his company. "I honestly was afraid," he said in an interview with Arthur T. Wilson for *Attitude* magazine's winter 1989 edition, "that modern dance traditions and techniques would fade into extinction . . . because of the lack of care and documentation. . . . I wished to preserve the techniques and styles of modern dance's tradition."

As early as 1960, Ailey began to seek out works by other choreographers to include in his company's repertoire—that body of work the company can perform.

From those, only some are used at any performance. The Ailey company has always been known for its versatility. Ailey kept in mind a need for variety as well as a desire to challenge his dancers when he selected or commissioned works for his company.

Concerned that great works would fade from memory and be lost to future generations, Ailey added popular works of the past and representative works of leading choreographers to his company's repertoire. In homage to his mentor, Lester Horton, he selected four of Horton's dances, and worked to keep alive the teaching of the Horton technique.

In 1987 Ailey dedicated an entire program to another great influence on his career, Katherine Dunham. Dunham's own *Choros* (1943) was already a part of the company's repertoire, but the full-evening program *The Magic of Katherine Dunham* was a special, emotional event for the performers and audience alike. Unfortunately, it is complex and expensive to mount, and so cannot be produced on a regular basis.

Preserving the works and traditions of black choreographers was always a major concern of Ailey, but important works by white choreographers also caught his attention. Looking toward the future, Ailey encouraged the efforts of young choreographers from both inside and outside his own company. Many Ailey company members and teachers have contributed works to the company's repertoire.

The Ailey company has dared to present new,

Alvin Ailey embraces the legendary Katherine Dunham, 1987. (Photo by Jack Vartoogian)

sometimes experimental works by current and emerging choreographers. These works do not have to reflect the black experience or the Horton tradition of movement. As long as they challenge the dancers to extend themselves in new ways, they can become part of the Ailey tradition. New dances give the audience an opportunity to see work on the cutting edge right next to tried and true favorites.

In addition to encouraging emerging choreographers, Ailey also encouraged and trained a new generation of dancers to perform their works. The Alvin Ailey American Dance Center, the official school of the Alvin Ailey American Dance Theater, grew from small beginnings in Brooklyn. Starting with about 150 students and one teacher, it is now an accredited institution serving more than 3,000 students each year and offering more than 150 classes per week.

The school has its own junior dance company, the Alvin Ailey Repertory Ensemble, which is sometimes called the second company. Created in 1974, not long after the company had become established in its third home, on Fifty-ninth Street, the second company aims to provide training for young dancers who are not yet ready for a full-time, professional career.

The Repertory Ensemble provides performance opportunities for young dancers who study at the American Dance Center. Some of the dancers go on to join the "first company"—the Alvin Ailey American Dance Theater—and some are invited to join other companies all over the world. The Repertory Ensemble also offers opportunities for Ailey dancers to try out their own choreography. Dances first performed by the second company sometimes find their way to the first company, where they may be seen by a wider audience. Other dances are later reworked or refined, and are sometimes performed by other modern-dance companies.

The artistic abilities of the dancers in the second company are not to be underestimated, but many dancers strive to make it to the first company. One 1990 program by the first company included a number of dancers—about half the company—who had progressed from student to Repertory Ensemble to first company.

Students at the American Dance Center come from all over the world as well as from across the United States. They study modern dance, including Graham, Dunham, and Horton techniques, as well as jazz, tap, and ballet. Advanced students study dance history, music, dance composition or choreography, theater arts, performing techniques, and partnering. They also learn dances from the Ailey repertory.

As an accredited institution, the American Dance Center can issue certificates of completion to students who successfully finish a two-year course of professional training. The process is much like going to a junior college. Students who have completed high school can audition to be admitted into the professional training programs. Auditions are held not only at the school but also in cities throughout the United States, so that the opportunity to study at the school will not be limited only to those who live near New York City. Scholarships are available for students who exhibit a promising level of talent or interest. Some spaces are reserved for teenagers who may not have had the benefit of early dance training but nevertheless exhibit a gift for dancing and, perhaps more important, have a strong desire to work and to learn. Foreign students may apply for student visas and join in the American Dance Center's Foreign Student Study Program.

Alvin Ailey, winner of the 1984 Monarch Awards, presented by the National Council for Culture & Art, Inc. Ailey is shown here with Dr. Robert La Prince, President of NCCA, and students of the Alvin Ailey American Dance Center school. (Courtesy of the National Council for Culture & Art, Inc.)

Students in the professional training programs leading to a certificate attend fourteen to fifteen classes per week and follow a rigorous curriculum with very high standards. Those who complete the program may be ready for the second company, or even for the first. Some will continue their studies as Merit Scholarship students, taking twelve to fifteen classes per week. Some exceptionally talented high school students are also admitted into the scholarship program.

The company has outreach programs in Kansas City and Baltimore, where two-week residency programs are held. During these residency programs, students in public schools have the opportunity to study with Ailey teachers, who are on the lookout for particularly talented dancers. There is also a summer residence camp, AileyCamp, in Kansas City.

In keeping with Ailey's original vision of making dance accessible to all, there are also classes at the school open to anyone who wants to come, from children through adults. Children may enter the Lower Division at age seven. They start off with beginning ballet and creative dance. They then progress to mime; pointe, or toe, work; tap dance; and the techniques of Horton, Graham, and Dunham. Through the age of fourteen, young students are carefully monitored by their teachers. Students must adhere to strict standards, progressing satisfactorily in dance and academic courses and following a very specific dress code in dance classes. Based on their teachers' evaluations and their own dreams of the future, some of these young students will be encouraged to audition for the High School of Performing Arts (now Fiorello H. La-Guardia High School of Music and Art and Performing Arts) or for an American Dance Center Merit Scholarship. Many go on to dance professionally, either with the Ailey company or one of the many other modern-dance companies in the United States or Europe. Only the most advanced students are selected for the Repertory Ensemble.

"WHEN GREAT TREES FALL"

On December 1, 1989, at the age of fifty-eight, Alvin Ailey, Jr., died of a rare blood disease. Since he had been ill for more than a year with dyscrasia, a blood disorder that affects the bone marrow and red blood cells, his death did not come as a surprise to his friends and colleagues. But it was still a shock and a loss to the dance world and to the nation.

Over the years Ailey had come to be known as a warm, giving, sometimes temperamental man. Always big for a dancer, in later years he was losing the battle over his growing waistline. An outstanding dancer, he turned his attention to nurturing a company that supported the dancing and choreography of other talented artists. His company and school reached thousands, introducing some to the world of dance for the first time, bringing others back to the theater again and again,

Alvin Ailey's brother,
Calvin Walls Cooper (left),
and mother (center) attend
his funeral, 1989. (Photo by
Hakim Mutlaq)

Dudley Williams dancing before Alvin Ailey's covered casket at his funeral,
1989. (Photo by Hakim Mutlaq)

Carmen de Lavallade speaking at Alvin Ailey's memorial service at the Cathedral of St. John the Divine, in New York City, 1989. (Photo by Hakim Mutlaq)

and inspiring a few to develop their own talents. In doing these things, Alvin Ailey, Jr., changed American modern dance forever and earned an honored place in history.

Ailey never got to see his company's newest home. The offices and studios at 211 West Sixty-second Street in New York City were dedicated while he was in the hospital. His mother came from California to attend the ceremony in his place.

Some 4,500 people attended Ailey's funeral and memorial service. "The Celebration of Alvin Ailey, Jr., Going Home" was held at the Cathedral of St. John the Divine. Speaking to the young dancers at the funeral, Ailey's friend and former partner Carmen de Lavallade said, "He gave you an open chest of gems, of jewels, and all you have to do is dip in your hand and take. Take it and use it and pass it on."

Judith Jamison also spoke: "He gave me legs until I could stand on my own as a dancer and a choreographer. He made us believe we could fly."

Writer Maya Angelou, reading from a poem written especially for the occasion, eulogized Ailey with these words: "When great trees fall, rocks on distant hills shudder. . . . Small things recoil into silence. . . . Lord, give him all the pliés he needs into eternity."

CHAPTER EIGHT

A SAMPLER OF AILEY DANCES

A lvin Ailey's adult life was centered in great part around dance. It is thus only fitting that some of his most important, best-loved dances be discussed at some length.

Said Ailey in the winter 1989 issue of *Attitude* magazine:

> *I wanted to express the richness of the early Black material of my life. . . . I wanted to trace folk songs and remnants of antiquity and connect them into a theatrical fabric. That became my first idea for the Company. That's the reason* Blues Suite *was on my first concert program. It was my first exploration into Black material. Two years later,* Revelations *was a reverberation of the same idea.*

Blues Suite (1958)

> *It remains one of Mr. Ailey's best pieces.*
> —Jack Anderson, *The New York Times*

> *With its burlesque humor and joyful tone, it seems a light work, yet it's underlaid with pathos.*
> —Kristy Montee, *Sun-Sentinel*, Fort Lauderdale, Florida

> *Ailey is not content to mourn without hope of celebration. . . . It is a work that not only stands out in Ailey's own choreographic canon, but one of the most effective, sincere tributes to an artist-friend in dance.*
> —Barton Wimble, *New York Daily News*

Many critics consider *Blues Suite*, Ailey's first major work, to be his second-best piece. The sounds and feelings of the blues are the inspiration for it. The "sporting house," or "bawdyhouse," is the setting. The women who work there are flashily dressed. They and their male customers are scattered about the stage, weighted down by the double burdens of Southern heat and social despair. The "Good Morning Blues" is their wake-up call. The music inspires them to stir, lazily at first. Each of the characters has an attitude. Then, in "Mean Ol' Frisco," a group of men perform a dance that allows them to express their feelings of frustration. The women are given a turn of their own with "House of the Rising Sun;" the lyrics and movements explore the feelings that led the women to a house of prostitution and what it is that made them stay. Throughout the dance, the men strut and swagger, but their bravado is all on the surface. It is clear that they are struggling to either deny or deal with their anger and dissatisfaction with their lives. The women sashay sassily and toss their feather boas, but beneath the glitter they, too, are hiding lost dreams. "In the Evening" finds them all getting ready to repeat the charade of their lives again.

Just like real life, the dance is not all about dejection and rejection. There are some light moments when the women flirt with the men, first pretending not to care about them, then changing their minds. One woman tries to be brighter and sexier and to get more attention than the others. She fails comically. The characters interact with anger, tenderness, love, and a whole range of familiar and recognizable emotions. It has a powerful effect on the audience. The return of "Good Morning Blues" is a signal that yet another day and night have gone by, and nothing has changed. Tomorrow, they will sing the blues yet again.

Music: Traditional folk music, Paquita Anderson, José Ricci. *Original scenery and costumes:* Geoffrey Holder. *First performance:* March 30, 1958, at the 92nd Street YM-YWHA, New York, NY. *Original cast: Dancers:* Julius Fields, Lavinia Hamilton, Tommy Johnson, Audrey Mason, Charles Moore, Charles Neal, Dorene

Richardson, Liz Williams, and Claude Thompson. *Singers:* Clarence Cooper and Nancy Reddy.

Revelations (1960)

> *Is there a more moving work in 20th century dance than* Revelations?
> —Richard Christiansen, *Chicago Tribune*

> *The singular masterpiece of the Ailey repertoire.*
> —Katie Gunther, *Baltimore Sun*

> *Powerful and eloquent dancing characterize the company in Ailey's timeless tribute to humanity, faith and survival.*
> —Clive Barnes, *New York Post*

> *Ailey's great masterpiece of 1960 [is a] tribute to the black heritage in America.*
> —Anna Kisselgoff, *The New York Times*

Revelations is the company's best known and most popular piece. Of the three major sections that originally made up the dance, two remain: "Pilgrim of Sorrow" and "Move, Members, Move." The work was changed a short time after its first performance. As the company grew larger, *Revelations* grew to include the new dancers.

Of the original sixteen songs, five are still part of the suite more than thirty years later. Some of the songs that Ailey originally found inspiring were elim-

The company in the opening of *Revelations*, at Alvin Ailey's funeral, 1989.
(Photo by Hakim Mutlaq)

inated or replaced with other, equally inspiring songs.
Ailey felt these new songs more accurately reflected his
vision and the growing technical skills of his dancers.
The work most recently included ten songs under
three major groupings: "Pilgrim of Sorrow," "Take Me
to the Water," and "Move, Members, Move." Some of
the songs added to the work, such as "Didn't My Lord
Deliver Daniel," "I Want to Be Ready," and "Rocka
My Soul in the Bosom of Abraham," have become audience favorites. Often, the audience is inspired to tap
their feet and clap along as they get caught up in the
spirit of an African-American church service. Perhaps
that is exactly what Ailey intended in choosing these
works.

"This suite," according to the original program,
"explores motivations and emotions of Negro religious

music which, like its heir the Blues, takes many forms." Later, some words of the poet Langston Hughes were added. They provided additional historical background while further explaining the artist's intent: "The Spirituals ask no pity for their words ride on the strongest of melodies, the melody of faith. That is why there is joy in their singing, peace in their music, and strength in their soul."

Revelations begins with the dancers clustered together in a group, in the center of the stage, arms stretched over their heads. This formation has been on posters all over the world. Even people who have never seen *Revelations* performed can identify the dance from pictures. But what is harder to see in a picture is the way the golden light streaming down from the ceiling frames the dancers. They appear to be bathed in a golden blessing from heaven.

The words to the introductory section—"I been 'buked, and I been scorn'd, children, I been talked about, sure as you're born"—tell the audience that this work is going to speak about triumph over difficulties. A person who can overcome "rebuke"—unjust criticism or oppression—must be a strong person, one who possesses great faith. This sentiment is reiterated in the following section, "Didn't My Lord Deliver Daniel?," which reminds us of the biblical tale of Daniel's rescue from the lion's den.

In a gentler mode, "Fix Me, Jesus" is a quiet prayer

of a dance for a man and woman—an adagio, in dance terminology. The duet makes a smooth transition into the middle section, "Take Me to the Water," which represents a symbolic baptism or ritual cleansing.

The "Processional" is a joyous occasion for a party dressed in white, under the direction of a woman bearing a large white umbrella. Many people will long remember Judith Jamison as the woman with the umbrella, but the umbrella has another historical significance as well. It was one of the props that Ailey developed a fondness for as a result of his apprenticeship with Lester Horton.

Two long strips of fabric are unfurled across the width of the stage and rise and fall like waves as the dancers step through the "water." Again taking its inspiration from the black church, this symbolic baptism leads to a search for ever-deepening faith. This search is symbolized in dance by a male soloist accompanied by the song "I Want to Be Ready." The man, aware of his sins, pleads in prayer for forgiveness and strength. He lifts his body upward from his reclining position, arms stretched toward heaven.

The highly energetic final section of the work starts off with three men running, sometimes on their knees, trying to hide from their sins or from the punishment for their sins. "Sinner Man" depicts the very human condition of men, aware of their shortcomings, promising to do better, and finding it extremely difficult to always do the right thing. The famous fan scene, "The Day Is Past and Gone," finds the women of the church dressed in their Sunday best, their wide-brimmed hats as much a fashion statement or a sign of their status as protection from the Southern summer sun. They enter fanning themselves against the heat and take their time greeting one another before settling down. The finale, "Rocka My Soul in the Bosom of Abraham," is both a spiritually powered conclusion to the suite and a purely physical release of emotion.

What makes this dance speak to people the world over, regardless of their particular situation or religious beliefs? People everywhere can identify with the universal themes of victory over adversity and of drawing strength from faith in God or another higher being. The situation for black people in America that created spirituals has been replicated in every society, for different reasons—political, economic, religious, racial. What Ailey tapped into with *Revelations* was not just African-American culture, but a common bond with all of humanity.

Music: Traditional spirituals. *First performance:* January 31, 1960, at the 92nd Street YM-YWHA, New York, NY. *Original cast:* Dancers: Joan Derby, Merle Derby, Jay Fletcher, Nathaniel Horne, Herman Howell, Minnie Marshall, and Dorene Richardson. *Singers:* Gene Hobgood and Nancy Reddy, with the Music Masters Guild Chorus of the Harlem Branch YMCA.

Hermit Songs (1961)

> *A dramatic little gem.*
> —Julinda Lewis, *Dance Magazine*

> Hermit Songs *is a celebration of robust manhood.*
> —Jennifer Dunning, *The New York Times*

Alvin Ailey created *Hermit Songs* for himself. While many of his dances were about the African-American experience, *Hermit Songs* was about the inner struggles of a cloistered medieval religious man, a European. It was set to songs by Samuel Barber, based on poems written by Irish monks and scholars from the eighth to the thirteenth centuries. The chanting of the sacred poems and the eerie and, to our ears, unfamiliar and ancient sound of the music, create a sense of distance and inspire a feeling of awe.

In the beginning of the dance, a monk in a dark, hooded robe begins to dance in a small circle. He is intent on his prayers or inner thoughts. As the dance develops, we see various and subtle aspects of the cleric's personality and motivation. There is tenderness, strength, humility, compassion, pain, uncertainty, questioning of faith. All of this is expressed in a tightly defined area of the stage, by a man whose body is mostly covered by a long robe. The dancer must use small gestures, subtle turns of the head and the merest hint of motion to create a very moving, powerful dance. After Ailey's death, *Hermit Songs* was revived

Alvin Ailey, with back to audience, rehearses Clive Thompson and Dudley Williams in the solo *Hermit Songs,* 1978. (Photo by Jack Vartoogian)

and performed by company member Gary DeLoatch, who received critical acclaim for the solo that Ailey had originally created for himself.

Music: Samuel Barber. *First performed:* 1961. *Original performer:* Alvin Ailey.

Masekela Langage (1969)

> *The anger of* Masekela Langage *takes the Ailey dancers beyond and out of their extraordinary physicality — which in and of itself is enough to mesmerize anyone.*
> —Laurie Horn, *The Miami Herald*

> Masekela Langage *has never been one of my favorites, but I like the atmosphere of a gaudy, seedy bar in Johannesburg. I like the anger and the restlessness, and I love watching the dancers.*
> —Deborah Jowitt, *The Village Voice*

Masekela Langage may be the best example of a dance expressing Ailey's social commitment and political consciousness. The work is choreographed to the music of the black South African trumpeter Hugh Masekela. Because of his anti-apartheid beliefs and his activities in pursuit of racial equality in his home country, Hugh Masekela spent some of his most creative years living in exile, like many other politically outspoken South African artists. (Many black South Africans

The company in *Masekela Langage*, 1980. (Photo by Jack Vartoogian)

found support and inspiration in the civil rights movement of American blacks.)

In *Masekela Langage* (not a misspelling of the word "language," but a Creole word meaning "a godly language intended for blacks"), Ailey attempted to capture in movement the heat of a black South African town, and the despair, anger, and frustration of the patrons of a black South African lounge. In some ways, the work is like *Blues Suite*. The settings are similar. Here, tropical lounge chairs are scattered about the bar, and a ceiling fan moves the hot air. And the people, though separated by thousands of miles from the characters in *Blues Suite*, are equally oppressed by racism and economic inequality. The men and women sit and stare into space. They stroll about aimlessly, their limbs weighted down. Everyday activities are interspersed with dance movements: Coins are put into a jukebox, which has to be kicked to get it started.

In spite of their problems and the apparent hopelessness of their situation, the people in *Masekela Langage* attempt to socialize; men and women flirt, have a party, carry on a normal life. As is often the case, their activities are interrupted by constant reminders of the pressures of the outside world. Most disturbing of all, the work climaxes as a bloodied and bandaged man, perhaps an anti-apartheid fighter, stumbles into the party, and dies. His entrance is a rude intrusion from the outside world, which the partygoers have tried hard to escape, if only for a few hours.

Unlike most popular Ailey dances, *Masekela Langage* is not slick, fast-paced, and smooth. It is raw, rough, almost unfinished, just like the buildings of the South African townships. The dancers move slowly, languidly, both because of the heat and because of the weight of their circumstances. The choreography is more a visualization of Masekela's trumpet playing than a narrative on its own. The feeling that is captured is summed up in the program note for this dance: "Looks like it's safer to be in jail."

Commissioned by Connecticut College American Dance Festival. *Music:* Hugh Masekela. *First performance:* Palmer Auditorium, Connecticut College, New London, Connecticut, August 16, 1969. *First New York City performance:* Brooklyn Academy of Music, November 21, 1969. *Cast of first New York City performance:* Kelvin Rotardier, Judith Jamison, George Faison, Renée Rose, John Medeiros, Sylvia Waters, Michele Murray.

Cry (1971)

If you haven't seen Cry, . . . *you haven't experienced one of the great moments in American dance.*
—Walter Terry, *Saturday Review*

Ailey choreographed many solos, but *Cry* was his best known. He created it as a tribute to his mother and dedicated it to "all Black women everywhere—especially our mothers." It quickly became a vehicle for showcasing the talents of the company's most outstanding women dancers. Leading soloist Judith Jamison was the first to perform *Cry*, and many consider it her greatest, most memorable role. Working closely with Ailey during the work's development gave Jamison a unique insight into his creative mind; after his death, this knowledge allowed her to carry on his artistic vision. *Cry* came to be closely associated with Jamison, but later it was performed by various other leading Ailey company dancers, including Sara Yarborough, Estelle Spurlock, and Donna Wood.

The dance is in three parts, each illustrating a different aspect of the struggles of African-American women. In the first section, the dancer unwinds a long white strip of fabric, which she will put to many uses as the dance develops: It becomes a headwrap, a shawl,

Donna Wood dances in
Alvin Ailey's *Cry*, 1983.

(Photo by Jack Vartoogian)

a sash, and, most memorably, a rag for washing the
floor and performing other domestic functions.

The first section of *Cry* is historical, briefly tracing
the role of the African-American woman in America
from slavery to the present. In the middle section, set
to Laura Nyro's somewhat mournful composition
"Been on a Train," the dancer turns her focus inward,
looking for meaning in all that has passed, or looking
for a source of strength to keep going in spite of past
hardships and disappointments. The soloist never stops
moving. The constant turning and African-derived
movements of the arms and torso are strenuous and

physically demanding. The third and last section is a vibrant reaffirmation of faith, set to the driving rhythm of "Right On, Be Free," sung by the Voices of East Harlem. This song was very much in tune with the political climate of the black community in the late 1960s and early 1970s. The dancer turns her attention away from the self-examination of the middle section to share her positive feelings, her joy, with the audience. The mood is infectious.

The music seemed to enhance the visual image, and when Judith Jamison performed *Cry*, audiences carried away long-lasting memories of her lithe, undulating torso. *Cry* is one of the dances that marked Ailey as a creative genius.

Music: Alice Coltrane, Laura Nyro, and Chuck Griffin. *First performance:* January 1971 at City Center Theater, New York City. *Original performer:* Judith Jamison.

Love Songs (1972)

> *It is very much a dancer's dance—something that depends entirely upon the talent of its performer to make the most of his material.*
> —Anna Kisselgoff, *The New York Times*

Ailey created *Love Songs* for Dudley Williams, who joined the company in 1964 and was still dancing in 1992, when he was much older than many dancers who had stopped performing. In *Love Songs*, Williams was required to bring his personal interpretation to the songs "A Song for You," "Poppies," and "He Ain't Heavy," sung by balladeers Donnie Hathaway and Nina Simone. Williams's fluid movements showed different aspects of loving relationships. The work was created for Williams because of his ability to express the essence of love, brotherhood, despair, longing, tenderness, and other feelings. With limited movement and a high degree of physical skill, Williams makes even the most difficult movement look easy.

When later performed by other dancers, such as company member Clive Thompson, the dance had a very different feeling. Ailey's choreography for this special solo adapts to the particular movement style and characteristics of the performer.

Music: Leon Russell, Jeremy Wind, Leonard Bleecher, Bobby Scott, and Bobby Russell. *First performed:* New York City, 1972. *Original performer:* Dudley Williams.

Memoria (1979)

A joyously lovely work.
> —Clive Barnes, *New York Post*

It's about the magnificence of dancing that springs from the core of the body and ripples outward, expanding to fill the stage and reaching out to touch the viewer.
> —Christine Temin, *Boston Globe*

Donna Wood leads the company in Ailey's *Memoria*, a tribute to his friend Joyce Trisler, 1980. (Photo by Jack Vartoogian)

A rhapsodic ensemble number that unfolds like the opening of a blossom.
— Alan M. Kriegsman, *The Washington Post*

In some ways, *Memoria* has a lot in common with *Revelations* and *Blues Suite*. Like these masterworks, *Memoria* was inspired by powerful, personal memories—in this case, Ailey's memories of his friend and colleague Joyce Trisler. Unlike such works as *Cry* or *Love Songs*, *Memoria* was not created to highlight the special qualities of any particular dancer. It has a lot in common with a work such as *Flowers*, a 1971 dance that captured the essence of singer Janis Joplin. But *Memoria* was different. Ailey's program note, in which he dedicated *Memoria* to "the joy . . . the beauty . . . the creativity . . . and the wild spirit of my friend Joyce Trisler," was both a sincere declaration of emotion and an accurate description of the work.

Joyce Trisler had studied with Lester Horton in Los Angeles and danced with the Horton company in the 1950s. She later became a leading teacher of the Horton technique, a close friend of Ailey, head of her own company, and an independent choreographer. Two of her works are in the Ailey repertoire: *Journey* (1958) and *Dance for Six* (1969). She died suddenly of a heart attack in October 1979.

Divided into two sections, *Memoria* was originally led by soloist Donna Wood, with Maxine Sherman alternating in the lead. The first section, "In Memory," has the leading dancer dressed, like Trisler in one of her own dances, in a long white dress, with a flower in her hair. The dance is a general tribute that anyone can understand, but there are specific references to Trisler and her works that only people familiar with them would recognize—for example, actual movement phrases from Trisler's own choreography, such as an arabesque and a hands-over-the-ears motif, both from Trisler's *Journey*. The female figure, who represents Trisler, is attended by two men who offer her symbolic as well as practical, physical support as she moves with quiet intensity toward the stage wings, where death awaits.

The second part of the work, "In Celebration," is a joyous mass of movement. The Trisler figure returns to the stage, clad in a defiantly bright red dress. With a stroke of genius that no doubt owes much to Ailey's and Trisler's common Horton heritage, Ailey fills the stage with more than thirty dancers, echoing Trisler's movement phrases, emphasizing Horton technique, and drawing the audience into the warm embrace of an outpouring of emotion. To accomplish this effect, Ailey had to use all twelve or so members of his company, the members of the Repertory Ensemble, and students from the American Dance Center Workshop.

Ten years after its first performance, the Ailey company included *Memoria* in its 1989 season. In the lead role of *Memoria* was a male dancer, Gary De-Loatch, dancing not the part of Joyce Trisler, but the part of Alvin Ailey, who had died just days before.

Music: Keith Jarrett. *First performance:* City Center 55th Street Theater, New York City, December 1979. *Original cast:* Donna Wood or Maxine Sherman; Gary DeLoatch and Alistair Butler, or Roman Brooks and Melvin Jones; Sarita Allen; Marilyn Banks; and members of the Alvin Ailey American Dance Theater, the Alvin Ailey Repertory Ensemble, and the American Dance Center Workshop.

BIBLIOGRAPHY

BOOKS

Beckford, Ruth. *Katherine Dunham: A Biography*. New York: Marcel Dekker, 1979.

Cook, Susan. *The Alvin Ailey American Dance Theater*. New York: William Morrow and Company, 1978.

Emery, Lynne Fauley. *Black Dance: From 1619 to Today*. 2nd, revised edition. Pennington, New Jersey: Princeton Book Company, 1988.

Haskins, James. *Black Dance in America*. New York: T. Y. Crowell, 1990.

Hodgson, Moira and Thomas Victor. *Quintet: Five American Dance Companies*. New York: William Morrow and Company, 1976.

Kuklin, Susan. *Reaching for Dreams*. New York: Lothrop, Lee & Shepard, 1987.

Maynard, Olga. *Judith Jamison: Aspects of a Dancer*. New York: Doubleday and Company, 1982.

McDonagh, Don. *Complete Guide to Modern Dance*. New York: Popular Library, 1977.

Probosz, Kathilyn Solomon. *Alvin Ailey, Jr.* New York: Bantam, 1991.

Thorpe, Edward. *Black Dance*. Woodstock, New York: The Overlook Press, 1990.

SELECTED ARTICLES

Barnes, Clive. "Alvin Ailey Dead at 58," *New York Post*, December 2, 1989, 8.

Dunning, Jennifer, "4,500 People Attend Ailey Memorial Service at St. John the Divine," *The New York Times* (obituary), December 9, 1989, 29.

Dunning, Jennifer. "Alvin Ailey: Believer in the Power of Dance," *The New York Times*, December 10, 1989, 30.

Gold, Sylviane. "The Ailey Generation," *Dance Magazine*, December 1988, 40–43.

Jowitt, Deborah. "Alvin Ailey, 1931–1989," *Village Voice* (obituary), December 12, 1989, 116.

Kisselgoff, Anna. "Alvin Ailey's Homage to Joyce Trisler," *The New York Times*, December 16, 1979, D16.

Moore, William. "Alvin Ailey (1931–1989)," *Ballet Review*, Winter 1990, vol. 17: 12–17.

Pacheco, Patrick. "The Book of Revelations: Alvin Ailey at the Precipice," *New York Daily News Magazine*, December 4, 1988, 10–11.

Pikula, Joan. "Celebrating Silver," *Dance Magazine*, December 1983, 44–49.

Todd, Arthur. "Roots of the Blues," *Dance and Dancers*, November 1961, 24–25.

Wilson, Arthur T. "Special Tribute to Alvin Ailey and the Alvin Ailey American Dance Theater On Its 30th Anniversary: A Million Roses Celebrating Champions," *Attitude*, Winter 1989, 37–75.

Zakariasen, Bill. "The Dance Is Over For Ailey," *New York Daily News*, December 2, 1989, 7.

SELECTED REVIEWS

Acocella, Joan. *7 Days*
—December 20, 1989, 82.

Berman, Janice. *New York Newsday*
   —December 7, 1990, 109.
   —December 17, 1990, 55.
   —December 20, 1990, 75.

Dionne, E. J. *The New York Times*
   —April 16, 1983, 13.

Dunning, Jennifer. *The New York Times*
   —May 14, 1978, 49.
   —December 3, 1979, C14.
   —December 9, 1979, 98.
   —December 21, 1986, 78.
   —December 11, 1990, C16.

Herridge, Frances. *New York Post*
   —November 26, 1978, 23A.

Kisselgoff, Anna. *The New York Times*
   —April 24, 1970, 43.
   —April 19, 1972, 37.
   —August 21, 1976, 12.
   —October 19, 1979, C12.
   —December 8, 1989, C3.

Wimble, Barton. *New York Daily News*
   —December 3, 1979, 31.

INDEX